Spotter's Guide to
INSECTS

Anthony Wootton
Illustrated by Phil Weare

with additional illustrations by Andy Martin

D1510554

Contents

Series Editor
Sue Jacquemier

Edited by
Jessica Datta

First published in 1979 by
Usborne Publishing Limited,
20 Garrick Street, London WC2

Text and Artwork © 1979 by
Usborne Publishing Limited

Printed in Great Britain

The name Usborne and the device ⬷ are
Trade Marks of Usborne Publishing Ltd.

How to use this book

This book is an identification guide to some of the insects of Britain and Europe. Take it with you when you go out spotting. There are more than 20,000 different species (or kinds) of insects in Britain alone, and the book includes only a selection of common and a few rarer ones.

Insects are divided scientifically into orders (butterflies and beetles are separate orders), and insects from all the main orders are included in the book. Some orders contain more kinds of insects than others and this is partly reflected in the book. For example, there are more moths shown than dragonflies or grasshoppers.

You may spot an insect that looks slightly different from one shown in the book. It may be the same species as the one shown but with its wings or body in another position, or it may be a different species related to the one shown. If you want to find out more about insects, there is a list of useful books and clubs on page 59.

The males and females of some species differ from each other. In these cases, both males and females are usually shown. The symbol ♂ means male, and ♀ means female. If the larva (caterpillar or nymph) is more commonly seen than the adult insect or is of particular interest, it is shown.

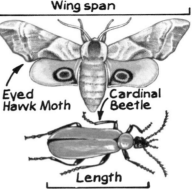

Wing span

Eyed Hawk Moth

Cardinal Beetle

Length

The description next to each insect tells you something about it – where it lives, where it lays its eggs and what it eats. If it says an insect lives in the south, it means the south of Britain. The description also gives you the insect's *approximate* adult length (not including the antennae) or wing span (W.S.). If the insect has been enlarged, the line next to the picture shows the actual size of the insect. All the other insects are drawn life size or a little smaller than life size.

You will find more information about insects at the end of the book, and the glossary on page 58 may also help you.

Scorecard
Next to each insect's description there is a blank circle. Make a tick in it when you spot the adult insect or its larva or pupa. The scorecard on page 60 gives you a score for each insect you spot. A common one scores 5 points, and a very rare one is worth 25. You can add up your score after a day out spotting.

	score	Date Seen
Agrion, Banded	15	
Agrion, Demoiselle	15	

Introducing insects

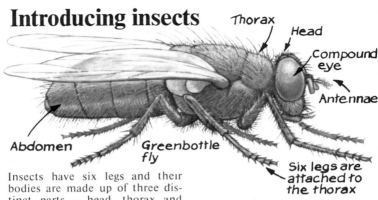

Thorax
Head
Compound eye
Antennae
Abdomen
Greenbottle fly
Six legs are attached to the thorax

Insects have six legs and their bodies are made up of three distinct parts – head, thorax and abdomen (although there are exceptions such as the silverfish). Many insects have one or two pairs of wings but in some, beetles for example, the wings are covered by hard wing cases and are not easy to see. Adult insects have a pair of antennae which they use for feeling and smelling, and two large compound eyes. Before becoming adult, insects pass through a complicated life cycle called "metamorphosis." This is explained on page 52. An insect larva and pupa (two of the stages in an insect's life cycle) may look very different from the adult insect.

These are not insects

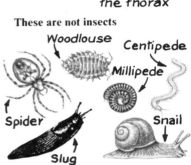

Woodlouse
Centipede
Millipede
Spider
Slug
Snail

The above are not insects. None of them have six legs or wings, and their bodies are not divided into three sections.

When and where to look
Insects can be found all year round, but summer is the best time. Look on flowers and leaves, in grass and soil, under stones, on tree bark, in water and even in houses.

You will find more species of insects on trees and in hedges than on garden flowers. Old oak trees, hedges where bramble and dog rose grow, and unpolluted ponds are places where many species live.

Some insects feed only on one kind of plant. These food plants will help you to identify the insect.

Keep your eyes open
Most insects are very small. Many fly or run fast and are coloured like the plants they live on. To be a successful insect spotter, you must train your eyes to look closely at the places where insects live. Don't try to cover too much ground at a time, but work slowly in a small area. Kneel or lie flat and look up at the undersides of leaves where insects may be hidden from the eyes of birds and other predators.

What to Take

When you go out spotting, it is important to take a notebook and pencil. Draw pictures of the insects you find and make notes about when and where you see them.

You can attract and catch insects in various ways, but remember that insects are fragile. Be careful when you handle them and try not to touch their wings. When you have looked carefully at each insect and made notes about it, let it go. Do not take insects home unless you are prepared to look after them properly (see page 56).

Matchboxes, sweet and tobacco tins and clear plastic sweet and slide boxes make very good insect containers. (Jam jars are heavy and bulky to carry.) Pick up insects very carefully and always put some grass or leaves into the container for them to cling to. This stops them being knocked about.

Lay a white sheet or a tray under a bush or hedge. Give the branches a sharp shake. Insects will fall on to the sheet.

To find insects that live underground, dig up soil with a small trowel or a spoon. The base of a tree is a good place to try this.

On a warm evening, paint a tree trunk with a mixture of treacle, beer and a drop of rum. Moths and other insects will be attracted by the sugar. This is called "sugaring".

You can make or buy a net for catching flying insects. Practise sweeping your net sideways and flipping it backwards to stop the insect from flying out. Be careful of stingers and biters.

Butterflies

Butterflies belong to the same order as moths, but unlike moths, all butterflies are daytime fliers. *Spotter's Guide to Butterflies* includes a larger selection of butterflies than appears in this book.

Wall Brown ▶

Dry open places and sunny walls and paths. Two broods each year in May-June and August. Larva eats meadow grass and other grasses.
W.S. 44-46 mm.

◀ Marbled White

Common on chalk in the south, but scarce or absent elsewhere. Dry grassy banks and disused railways. Lays eggs on grasses.
W.S. 53-58 mm.

Pearl-bordered Fritillary ▶

Likes dog rose and wood violet flowers in woodland clearings. Lays eggs on violet. All over Britain, but most common in the south.
W.S. 42-46 mm.

Male's wings have less black

♀

◀ Holly Blue

Open woodland and gardens with tall holly trees. Larva eats flower buds of holly and ivy. Most common in south and east England.
W.S. 33-35 mm.

Butterflies

Purple Hairstreak ▶

Flies round tops of oak trees. Like all Hairstreaks, larva is slug-like, but not slimy. Brownish larva eats oak leaves.
W.S. 36-39 mm.

Male has more purplish blue on the wings

♀

◀ Clouded Yellow

Sometimes arrives in spring from south Europe. Breeds here and lays eggs on clover and lucerne, but larvae do not survive our winters.
W.S. 58-62 mm.

Brimstone ▶

Common, but not found in Scotland. Female is pale greeny-white. Larva eats leaves of buckthorn. Notice shape of wings.
W.S. 58-60 mm.

♂

Peacock ▶

Gardens in spring and late summer. Adults hibernate in winter, often in houses. Bristly black larva has tiny white spots, and eats nettles.
W.S. 62-68 mm.

Moths

Most moths are nocturnal, which means they are active at night. Moths' antennae are not club-ended like those of butterflies.

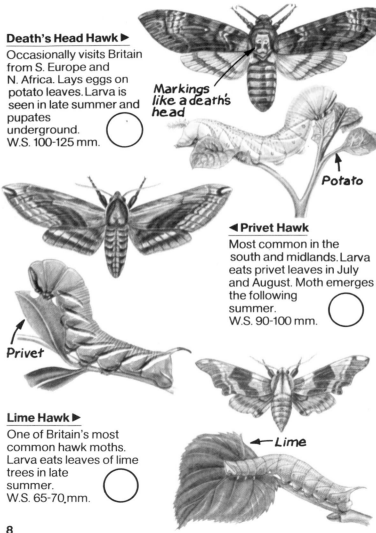

Death's Head Hawk ▶

Occasionally visits Britain from S. Europe and N. Africa. Lays eggs on potato leaves. Larva is seen in late summer and pupates underground. W.S. 100-125 mm.

Markings like a death's head

Potato

◀ Privet Hawk

Most common in the south and midlands. Larva eats privet leaves in July and August. Moth emerges the following summer. W.S. 90-100 mm.

Privet

Lime Hawk ▶

One of Britain's most common hawk moths. Larva eats leaves of lime trees in late summer. W.S. 65-70 mm.

Lime

Moths

Eyed Hawk ▶

Flashes markings on its underwings to frighten birds and other enemies. Larva feeds on sallow and leaves of plum and apple trees. W.S. 75-80 mm.

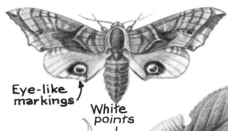

Eye-like markings

White points

Apple

◀ Poplar Hawk

Common all over Britain. Larva feeds on poplar or sallow and, like Eyed Hawk, has rough skin surface. Notice yellow markings. W.S. 75-80 mm.

Yellow points

Poplar

Hummingbird Hawk ▶

Visitor to Britain. Gardens during day. Hovers over flowers to feed, beating its wings like a hummingbird. Lays eggs on bedstraw. W.S. 45 mm.

Bedstraw

Moths

Elephant Hawk ▶

Widespread, but scarce in Scotland. Larva tapers at head end like an elephant's trunk. It feeds on willowherb and bedstraw.
W.S. 65 mm.

Willowherb

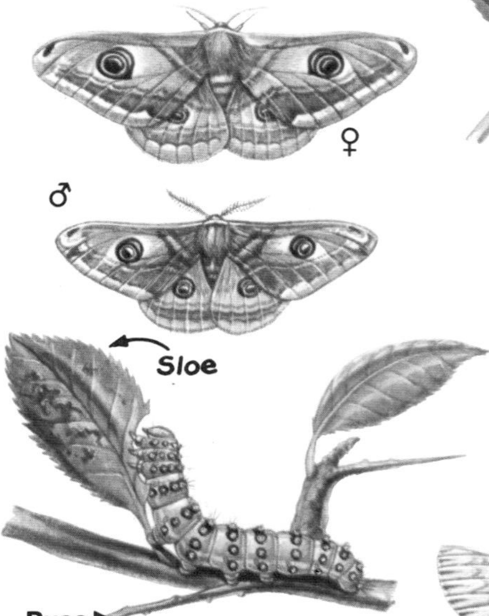

♀

♂

Sloe

◀ Emperor

All over Britain. Male flies by day over moorland, looking for female which comes out at dusk. Lays eggs on heather, bramble, etc. Appearance of larva changes when each skin is shed.
W.S. female
70 mm.
Male 55 mm.

Puss ▶

Widespread in Britain. Lays eggs, usually singly, on willow or sallow in May-June. Thin red "whips" come out of larva's tails, perhaps to frighten birds.
W.S. 65-80 mm.

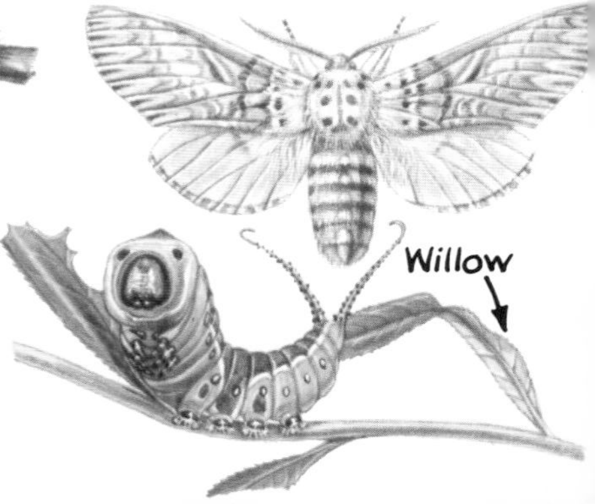

Willow

Moths

Lobster ▶

S. England, Wales and parts of S. Ireland. Name comes from the shape of the larva's tail end. Larva eats beech. W.S. 65-70 mm.

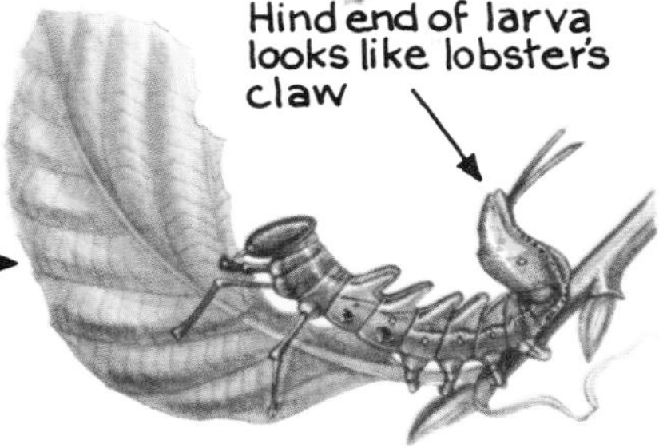

Hind end of larva looks like lobster's claw

Beech

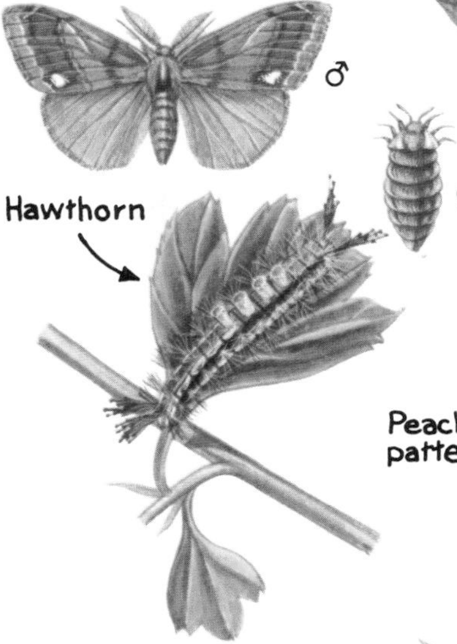

♂

Hawthorn

♀

◀ Vapourer

Common all over Britain, even in towns. Female has only wing stubs and cannot fly. Larva feeds on a variety of trees. W.S. 35 mm.

Peach blossom pattern

Peach Blossom ▶

Found in woodland. Name comes from pattern on wings. Often attracted by "sugaring" (see page 5). Larva feeds on bramble. W.S. 35 mm.

Bramble

Moths

◀ Yellow-tail
Brightly coloured larvae
are often found in
hedgerows of hawthorn,
sloe and bramble
in May and June.
W.S. 32-40 mm.

Hawthorn

Merveille-du-Jour

Merveille-du-Jour ▶
Oak woodlands. Forewings
match background of tree
bark making moth difficult
for enemies to see.
Larva eats
oak leaves.
W.S. 45 mm.

Oak

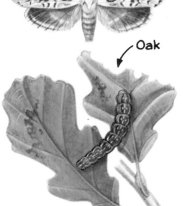

Alder
Moth

Alder

◀ Alder
Like many other species,
the larva is more striking
than the adult moth. It
feeds on a variety of trees,
including alder
and oak.
W.S. 37 mm.

Moths

Clifden Nonpareil or Blue Underwing ▶

Breeds in a few places in Kent, but sometimes visits other parts of Britain, usually in late summer. Stick-like larva feeds on black poplar and aspen. W.S. 90 mm.

Colour of upper wings matches tree bark

◀ Red Underwing

Quite common in south and midlands. Flashes underwings when threatened by birds. Rests in daytime on trees. Larva eats poplar and willow. W.S. 80 mm.

Larva of Red Underwing

Willow

Face-like markings on wings

Mother Shipton ▶

Flies on bright sunny days. Look on railway banks and in meadows in May and June. Larva eats vetches and clover. Mother Shipton was a seer who lived from 1488-1561. W.S. 35 mm.

Clover

Larva of Mother Shipton

Moths

Y-shaped marking

◄ Silver Y

Visitor to Britain, some years in great numbers. Feeds on garden flowers with long proboscis. Flies fast. Larva eats nettle, thistle, etc. W.S. 40 mm.

Herald ►

Widespread in Britain. Hibernates during the winter in barns, sometimes in small groups. Mates in spring and female lays eggs on various kinds of willow. W.S. 40 mm.

Larva of Herald

Willow

This is Northern Eggar, more common in north of England and Scotland

Female is larger and paler ♂

◄ Oak Eggar

Male flies by day searching for female who rests in heather on moorland. Larva eats heather, bramble, hawthorn, etc. W.S. 50-65 mm.

Hawthorn

Moths

Lappet ▶

Name comes from "lappets" on larva. Feeds on apple, sallow and hawthorn. Adult's brown colour, ragged wing edges and veined wings make it look like a bunch of leaves.
W.S. 60-70 mm.

Projection or lappet

Sallow

Wing pattern varies

◀ Wood Tiger

Smaller and more local than Garden Tiger. Widespread on hillsides, heaths and open woodland. Larva eats violets and forget-me-nots, and hibernates.
W.S. 35-40 mm.

Plantain

Garden Tiger ▶

Common, but larva more often seen. Feeds on many low-growing plants and hibernates when young. Feeds again in spring and is fully grown by June.
W.S. 60-70 mm.

Larva is called "woolly bear"

Moths

Cinnabar ▶

Sometimes flies by day, but weakly. Striped larvae feed in groups on ragwort. Common on waste ground and railway banks.
W.S. 40-45 mm.

Ragwort

Larva inside tree trunk

◀ Goat

Widespread, but well camouflaged and rarely seen. Larva eats wood of ash and willow. Spends three or four years in a tree trunk and pupates in a silk-bonded cocoon made of wood shavings. Larva smells like goats.
W.S. 70-85 mm.

Swallow-tailed ▶

Looks like a butterfly. Weak, fluttering flight. Stick-like larva feeds on leaves of ivy, hawthorn, sloe, etc.
W.S. 56 mm.

Moths

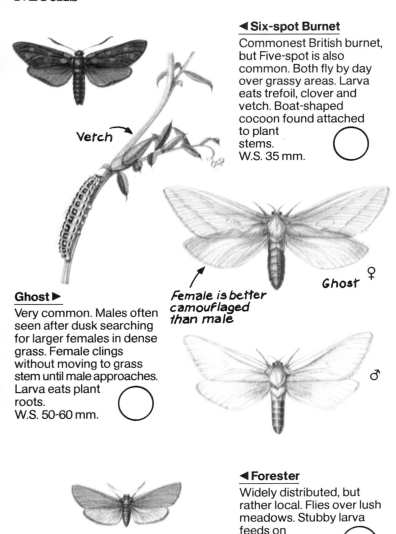

◀ Six-spot Burnet

Commonest British burnet, but Five-spot is also common. Both fly by day over grassy areas. Larva eats trefoil, clover and vetch. Boat-shaped cocoon found attached to plant stems.
W.S. 35 mm.

Vetch

Ghost ♀

Female is better camouflaged than male

Ghost ▶

Very common. Males often seen after dusk searching for larger females in dense grass. Female clings without moving to grass stem until male approaches. Larva eats plant roots.
W.S. 50-60 mm.

♂

◀ Forester

Widely distributed, but rather local. Flies over lush meadows. Stubby larva feeds on sorrel.
W.S. 25-27 mm.

Beetles

Most beetles have a pair of hard wing cases called elytra. There are several thousand species of beetles in Europe and their size varies enormously.

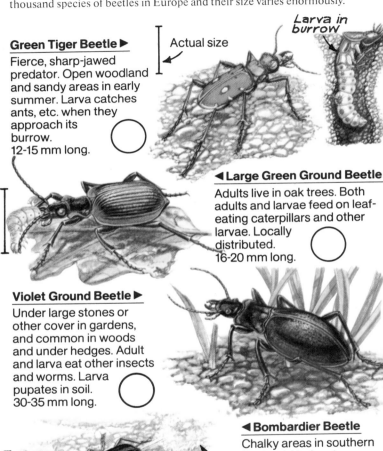

Green Tiger Beetle ▶

Fierce, sharp-jawed predator. Open woodland and sandy areas in early summer. Larva catches ants, etc. when they approach its burrow.
12-15 mm long.

Actual size

Larva in burrow

◀ Large Green Ground Beetle

Adults live in oak trees. Both adults and larvae feed on leaf-eating caterpillars and other larvae. Locally distributed.
16-20 mm long.

Violet Ground Beetle ▶

Under large stones or other cover in gardens, and common in woods and under hedges. Adult and larva eat other insects and worms. Larva pupates in soil.
30-35 mm long.

Gas shooting from abdomen

◀ Bombardier Beetle

Chalky areas in southern England. Under stones. Shoots irritating gas from end of its abdomen with a popping sound when threatened.
7-10 mm long.

Beetles

Devil's Coach Horse or Cocktail Beetle ▶

Common in gardens. When challenged, raises tail and spreads jaws. Can ooze poisonous liquid from end of abdomen. Eats insect larvae, snails, slugs, etc. 25-30 mm long.

Larva

◀ Rove Beetle

Feeds mainly on dead animals and birds. Most common in southern England. Related to Devil's Coach Horse. 20 mm long.

Red and Black Burying Beetle ▶

Feeds on dead animals, kneading and biting the flesh and then burying the body. Female lays eggs in burrow beside the body. Larvae feed on it and pupate in a chamber in soil. 15-20 mm long.

Mouse

◀ Ant Beetle

Small, fast-moving beetle found on elms and conifers. Larvae live under loose bark. Adults and larvae eat larvae of bark beetles. 7-10 mm long.

Beetles

Great Diving Beetle ▶

Lakes and large ponds. Eats tadpoles, small fishes and other insects. Collects air from surface and stores it between wing covers and end of abdomen. 30-35 mm long.

Male's wing cases are smoother than female's

Larva

◀ Great Silver Water Beetle

Largest British water beetle. Eats mainly water plants, but larva is a predator and eats water snails. Can fly to other waters if its home dries up. 37-48 mm long.

Carries bubble of air under body ⤴

Whirligig Beetle ▶

Seen in groups on surface of ponds, lakes and slow rivers in bright sunshine. Darts in all directions. Carnivorous, eating mosquito larvae, etc. 6-8 mm long.

◀ Water Beetle

Lives among vegetation of lakes and rivers where it lays its eggs. Colour may be darker, sometimes all black. Widespread. 7-8 mm long.

Beetles

Glow-worm ▶

Grassy banks, hillsides, open woods. Most common in S. England. Wingless female attracts male with her glowing tail.
Male 15 mm long.
Female 20 mm long.

♀

Larva

♂

◀ Lesser Glow-worm

Near streams and on damp grassy banks. Like Glow-worm, male and larva have small lights on tip of abdomen. C. and S. Europe, but not found in Britain.
8-10 mm long.

♀

♂

Scarlet-tipped Flower Beetle ▶

Most common in southern England. In buttercups and other flower heads. Blows up scarlet bladders on its underside when handled.
7-10 mm long.

Buttercup

Larva is called "wireworm"

◀ Click Beetle or Skipjack

Local in dense vegetation or in flowers. Larvae live in soil, eating plant roots; other species of click beetle do much damage to crops.
14-18 mm long.

Larva

Beetles

Two-spot Ladybird ▶
Very common. Colour pattern often varies and some individuals are shiny black with red spots. 4-5 mm long.

Ladybird eating aphid

Rose

◀ Seven-spot Ladybird
Very common. Hibernates in large numbers in sheds, houses or tree bark. Emerges on sunny spring days to find aphids and lay its eggs. 6-7 mm long.

Eyed Ladybird ▶
Largest ladybird in Britain. Found near or on fir trees. Both adults and larvae hunt for aphids and scale-insects. 8-9 mm long.

Fir

Pattern varies

◀ 22-spot Ladybird (left)
◀ 14-spot Ladybird (right)
22-spot is found in many areas and habitats. 2-3 mm long. 14-spot is rare in the north. Trees and bushes. 3-4 mm long.

Beetles

Death Watch Beetle ▶
Larva eats timber in barns. The sound the adult makes when it taps its head against its tunnel walls was once believed to predict a death.
7-10 mm long.

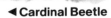

◀ Cardinal Beetle
One of three species of cardinal beetles found in Britain. On flowers and under bark. Whitish larvae feed on bark and wood.
15-17 mm long.

Oil Beetle ▶
Flightless. Larva waits in a flower for a special kind of solitary bee to carry it to its nest where the larva feeds and grows. Local.
15-30 mm long.

◀ Blister Beetle
Rare. Name comes from a fluid in the insect's blood which causes blisters on human skin. Larvae live in mining bees' nests as parasites.
12-20 mm long.

Beetles

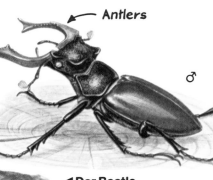

Antlers

♂

Stag Beetle ▶

Largest British beetle. Only male has antlers. Larvae feed on tree stumps for three years or more. Most common in the south, particularly Kent and Surrey. 25-75 mm long.

◀ Dor Beetle

Common. Seen flying at night to dung heaps where it lays its eggs. Makes a loud droning sound when it flies. 16-24 mm long.

Horned Dung Beetle or Minotaur Beetle ▶

In sandy places where rabbits live. Eats their dung and fills tunnels with it for larvae to eat. Local. 12-18 mm long.

◀ Cockchafer or May Bug

Common. Flies round tree tops in early summer and sometimes down chimneys and at lighted windows. Larvae may be dug up in gardens. 25-30 mm long.

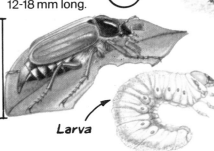

Larva

24

Beetles

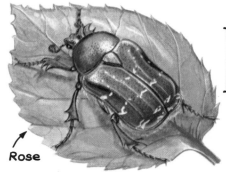

Rose Chafer ▶

Sometimes found in rose blooms and other flowers. Larvae feed on old timber and roots. Found all over Britain, but localized. 14-20 mm long.

Rose

Hairy like a bee

Pignut

◀ Bee Beetle

Mainly in Scotland and Wales. Found in flowers. Mimics colouring of bees (see page 55). Larvae eat rotting wood, especially birch. 10-13 mm long.

Long "horns"

Musk Beetle ▶

Longhorn beetles have long antennae, perhaps so they can recognize each other when they emerge from their pupae in wood tunnels. 20-32 mm long.

Willow

◀ Wasp Beetle

Harmless, but looks and behaves like a wasp. Flies in bright sunshine visiting flowers. Common throughout Britain. 15 mm long.

Beetles

Colorado Beetle ▶

Damages potato crops.
Introduced by accident
from America; some still
appear from Europe. Tell
the police if
you spot one.
10-12 mm long.

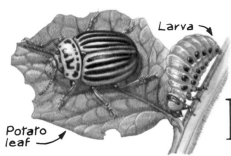

Larva

Potato
leaf

◀ Bloody-nosed Beetle

Like Oil and Blister Beetles,
it reacts when threatened.
It spurts bright red fluid
from its mouth. This is
called "reflex-bleeding".
Low dense
foliage.
10-20 mm long.

Green Tortoise Beetle ▶

Legs and antennae often
hidden so it looks like a
tortoise. Well camouflaged
on thistles where it feeds,
and where
larvae pupate.
6-8 mm long.

Mint

Fork
in larva
tail holds
shed skins
and droppings

◀ Nut Weevil

Female uses her long
rostrum (or snout) to
pierce a young hazel-nut
where she lays her single
egg. Larva grows inside
the nut, eating
the kernel.
10 mm long.

Long
rostrum

Larva inside
hazelnut

Bugs

Bugs might be confused with beetles, but their mouthparts are different. Bugs have a tube called a rostrum for piercing and sucking; beetles' mouthparts are adapted for biting, cutting and chewing.

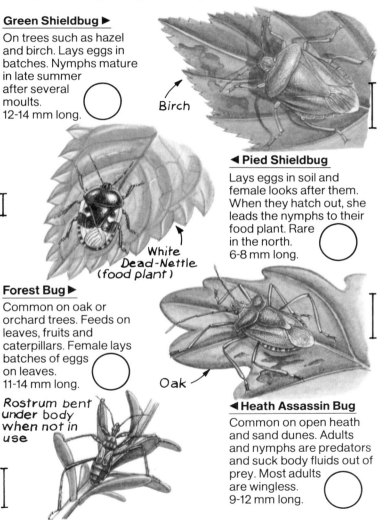

Green Shieldbug ▶

On trees such as hazel and birch. Lays eggs in batches. Nymphs mature in late summer after several moults.
12-14 mm long.

Birch

◀ Pied Shieldbug

Lays eggs in soil and female looks after them. When they hatch out, she leads the nymphs to their food plant. Rare in the north.
6-8 mm long.

White Dead-Nettle (food plant)

Forest Bug ▶

Common on oak or orchard trees. Feeds on leaves, fruits and caterpillars. Female lays batches of eggs on leaves.
11-14 mm long.

Oak

Rostrum bent under body when not in use

◀ Heath Assassin Bug

Common on open heath and sand dunes. Adults and nymphs are predators and suck body fluids out of prey. Most adults are wingless.
9-12 mm long.

27

Bugs

Water Cricket ▶

Common on still and slow-moving water. Runs on water surface eating insects and spiders. Lays eggs out of water on moss.
6-7 mm long.

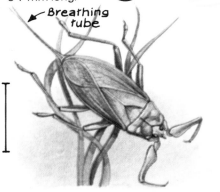

← Breathing tube

◀ Water Scorpion

Ponds and shallow lakes. Seizes small fishes, tadpoles, insect larvae with forelegs. Lays eggs in algae or on water plants.
18-22 mm long.

Water Stick Insect ▶

Not related to true stick insects, but like them it is hard to see among plants. Most common in south Wales and southern England.
30-35 mm long.

◀ Water Measurer

Edges of ponds and slow rivers and streams. Stabs at mosquito and larvae and water fleas with its rostrum. Also eats dead insects.
9-12 mm long.

Bugs

Water Boatman
or Backswimmer ▶

Pools, canals, ditches and water tanks. Jerks along with its hind legs, usually on its back. Eats tadpoles, small fishes, etc. Can fly away if its home dries up.
15 mm long.

Boat-like keel

Breathes from tail end

◀ Lesser Water Boatman

Flatter and rounder than Water Boatman and has shorter legs. Sucks up small bits of animal and plant material at bottom of ponds.
Common.
12-14 mm long.

Pond Skater ▶

Front legs adapted to catch dead or dying insects that fall on water surface. Some can fly; others have no wings. Common in ponds.
8-10 mm long.

◀ Saucer Bug

Lives in vegetation at bottom of muddy pools and canals. Like the Water Boatman it can stab you with its rostrum. Hibernates in winter as do most water bugs.
12-16 mm long.

29

Bugs

New Forest Cicada ▶

Male makes high-pitched buzzing sound that is very difficult to hear. Nymphs live underground for several years eating plant roots. The only British cicada. 25 mm long.

Adult sucks sap from trees

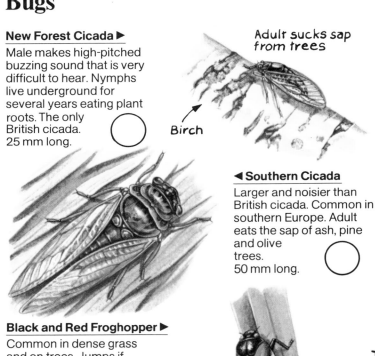

Birch

◀ Southern Cicada

Larger and noisier than British cicada. Common in southern Europe. Adult eats the sap of ash, pine and olive trees. 50 mm long.

Black and Red Froghopper ▶

Common in dense grass and on trees. Jumps if disturbed. Larvae secrete froth which covers them when they feed underground. 9-10 mm long.

Bracken

◀ Horned Treehopper

Tree branches and low vegetation, such as bracken, in woods. Adult and larva feed on oak leaves and other plants. 9-10 mm long.

Bugs

Eared Leafhopper ▶

On lichen-covered oak or other trees where it is well hidden. Adults appear about June. Moves slowly. Local in southern England. 13-17 mm long.

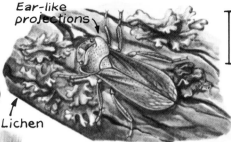

Ear-like projections

Lichen

◀ Green Leafhopper

Common throughout Britain. Feeds on grasses and rushes often in damp meadows and marshy places. 6-9 mm long.

Rose Aphid or Greenfly ▶

Green or pinkish. Feeds on roses in spring, then moves to other plants. Excretes honeydew which ants feed on. Pest on roses. 2-3 mm long.

Rose

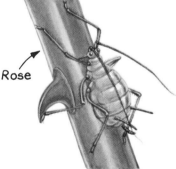

◀ Bean Aphid or Blackfly

Common on broad bean, but also on thistle and other plants. Lays eggs on spindle trees. Adults from these produce fully-formed young which eat beans. 2-3 mm long.

31

Dragonflies and Damselflies

Hawker dragonflies fly fast and hover and turn in the air. Darters fly in short, sharp bursts. Dragonflies, damselflies and their nymphs are carnivorous. They have very large compound eyes for spotting prey.

Emperor Dragonfly ▶

Largest British hawker. Large ponds, lakes and canals in summer. Adult catches flies, etc. in flight.
W.S. 105 mm.
80 mm long.

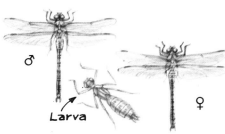

♂

Larva

♀

◀ Golden-ringed Dragonfly

Near streams and rivers, but like many dragonflies it is sometimes seen far from water. Female lays eggs in mud.
W.S. 100 mm.
75-85 mm long.

Female is longer than male

♂

Broad-bodied Libellula ▶

Ponds and lakes, particularly in southern England. Darters have shorter wings and stubbier bodies than hawkers. They fly in short sharp bursts.
W.S. 75 mm.
45 mm long.

♂

♀

◀ Downy Emerald

This darter flies fast over sluggish streams, rivers, ponds and lakes in summer. Quite common in S. England.
W.S. 68 mm.
48 mm long.

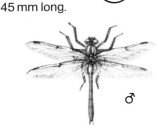

♂

Dragonflies

Ruddy Sympetrum ▶

Weedy ponds or ditches
in marshy areas. Nymphs
mature more quickly than
the larger dragonflies
which may take
2-3 years.
W.S. 55 mm.
35 mm long.

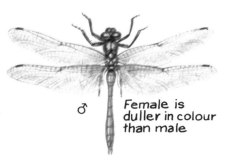

♂   *Female is
duller in colour
than male*

♂

◀ Demoiselle Agrion

Fast-flowing clear streams
with sandy or stony
bottoms. Damselflies
usually rest with wings
together, not spread out
like dragonflies.
W.S. 58-63 mm.
45 mm long.

♀

♂

Banded Agrion ▶

More common than the
Demoiselle but rare in
northern England and not
recorded from Scotland.
Usually by streams and
rivers with
muddy bottoms.
W.S. 60-65 mm.
45 mm long.

♀

♂

◀ Common Ischnura or
Blue-tailed Damselfly

On plants by ditches,
canals, lakes, ponds and
slow-moving rivers and
streams. Common in most
of Britain.
W.S. 35 mm.
30 mm long.

Bees and Wasps

Bees, wasps and ants belong to the same order. Some species are "social insects" and colonies of these include queens, drones and workers. Other insects in this order are solitary and have no caste system.

Red-tailed Bumblebee ▶

Common in gardens. Queen makes a nest in a hole in the ground. Eggs develop into colonies of queens, workers and drones. Queen is 22 mm long.

Nest

Leaves cut by bee

◀ Leaf-cutter Bee

Cuts semi-circular pieces from rose leaves to make cylinders where the female lays a single egg provided with nectar and pollen. Solitary species. Male 10 mm long. Female 11 mm.

Potter Wasp ▶

Makes pots of clay for its larvae. Each larva has a separate pot, stocked with small caterpillars (paralyzed with a sting) for food. Sandy heaths. Male 12 mm long. Female 14 mm.

Pot

◀ Sand Wasp

Makes a nest burrow in sand where it lays a single egg on top of a paralyzed caterpillar. Larva eats the caterpillar. 28-30 mm long.

Wasps

Ruby-tailed Wasp ▶

Called a "cuckoo-wasp" because female lays egg in nest of a solitary bee or wasp. When larva hatches it eats host's food and its egg or larva. 12 mm long.

◀ Velvet Ant

Actually a wasp, but female is wingless. She lays her egg in a bee larva which is eaten by her own larva when it hatches. Can sting painfully. 15 mm long.

♀

Ichneumon Fly ▶

A wasp, not a fly. Female pierces pine trees with her ovipositor (egg layer) and lays an egg on a Horntail larva or in its burrow inside the tree. 22-30 mm long.

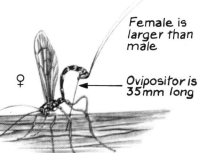

Female is larger than male

♀

Ovipositor is 35mm long

♂

◀ Giant Wood Wasp or Horntail

Female lays eggs in sickly or felled conifers. Larvae feed on wood for up to three years. 25-32 mm long.

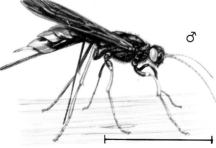

Wasps

Blue Horntail ▶

Male like male Horntail except his head, thorax and the first two segments of his abdomen are deep metallic blue. Female is all blue and has only a short ovipositor. 20-25 mm long.

Dog rose

◀ Hornet

Not as likely to sting as the Common Wasp. Nests in hollow trees, banks or roofs. Preys on soft-bodied insects with which it feeds its larvae. Also feeds from flowers in woods. 22-30 mm long.

Brown and yellow markings

German Wasp ▶

With the Common Wasp, Britain's commonest species. Most troublesome in late summer when the larvae are mature. 15-20 mm long.

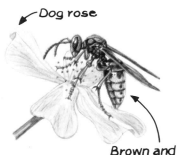

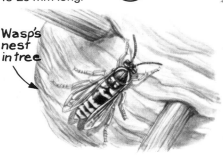

Marmalade

◀ Tree Wasp

Likes to nest in woods, often hanging its oval nest from a tree branch. More locally distributed than Common or German Wasps. 15-20 mm long.

Wasp's nest in tree

Ants

Carpenter Ant ▶

Hollows out pine tree trunks where it nests, often making the tree fall down.
Not in Britain.
8-18 mm long.

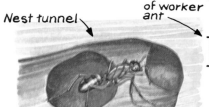

Actual size of worker ant

Nest tunnel

◀ Wood Ant

Makes large conical nest from twigs and leaves in pine woods. Useful to foresters as it eats leaf-eating larvae. Cannot sting, but sprays formic acid at intruders.
5-11 mm long.

Nest

Red Ant ▶

Nests under stones or in rotting wood. Rears aphids in its nest and feeds on their honeydew.
3-6 mm long.

Nest in tree stump

◀ Black Ant

Common in gardens. Like all ants, only queens and males have wings. Males die after mating and queens start a new colony.
3-9 mm long.

Ant, Sawfly, Gall-wasps

Yellow Meadow Ant ▶

Makes small mounds in meadows. Sometimes "farms" other small insects, such as aphids, for a sugary liquid that they excrete. 2-9 mm long.

I

Actual size of worker ant

Sawfly larva has nine pairs of legs. Moth larvae have eight pairs

◀ Birch Sawfly

Name "sawfly" comes from female's saw-like ovipositor. Larva feeds on birch leaves in late summer. It makes a large oval cocoon and the adult emerges the next spring. 20-23 mm long.

Marble gall

Oak Marble Gall-wasp ▶

Female lays egg in leaf bud. Larva's feeding causes the tree to "blister" round it. Only one larva lives in each "marble". 4 mm long.

I

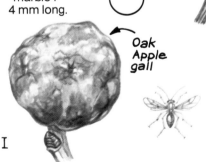

Oak Apple gall

◀ Oak Apple Gall-wasp

These galls can be 40 mm across and are at first red and green and then later darken. Each gall contains many larvae. Insect is 3 mm long.

I

38

True Flies

True flies have only one pair of wings. The second pair are replaced by two halteres which are like tiny drumsticks. Flies probably use them for balance.

The insects that appear on pages 42–44 are not true flies, but belong to different orders.

Grey Flesh Fly ▶

Common. Lays eggs in carrion. White, legless larvae (maggots) feed on flesh before turning into oval brown pupae.
6-17 mm long.

Rat

◀ Greenbottle Fly

Most species lay eggs in carrion. Adults seen on flowers. One species lays eggs in skin or fleece of sheep and its larvae eat the sheep's flesh.
7-11 mm long.

Mouse ➤

Drone Fly ▶

Makes a loud, bee-like droning in flight. Visits flowers for nectar and pollen. Larva rests on the pond bottom and breathes through a long tube.
15 mm long.

Breathing tube

Antirrhinum

◀ Hover Fly

Hovers as though motionless. Common in summer. Female lays eggs among aphids and the legless larvae eat them.
10-14 mm long.

True Flies

Dung Fly ▶

Visits fresh cowpats where female lays eggs. Rise in a buzzing mass if disturbed but soon settle again. Larvae eat dung but adults are predators on other flies. 10-12 mm long.

Cow pat

Robber-fly killing damsel fly

◀ Robber Fly

Preys on other insects by capturing them and sucking out their body fluids. Larvae feed on animal dung as well as vegetable matter. 18-26 mm long.

Bee Fly ▶

Probes flowers in gardens for nectar in spring. Lays eggs near nests of mining bees and its larvae eat the bee's larvae. Most common in S. England. 10-11 mm long.

Sweet woodruff

Piercing arm

◀ Horse Fly

Female sucks blood but her loud hum warns you before you get bitten. Smaller species are more silent and stab before being noticed. Found in old forests in S. England. 20-25 mm long.

True Flies

Fever Fly ▶

Does not bite or cause fever. Most noticeable in spring and summer. Males perform courtship dance in the air above females. 8 mm long.

Water violet

◀ Giant Cranefly or Daddy-long-legs

Often near water. Other species found in gardens where larvae (called "leatherjackets") eat root crops and grass roots. 30-40 mm long.

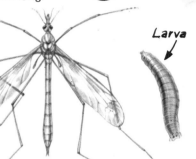

Larva

Black and Yellow Cranefly ▶

Low vegetation. Craneflies mate end to end and can be seen joined like this in summer. Female lays eggs in soil with her pointed ovipositor. 18-20 mm long.

◀ Common Gnat or Mosquito

Female sucks people's blood. Lays eggs in raft-like clusters which float on water. Larvae hang down below surface. 6-7mm long.

Water surface

41

Ant-lion, Lacewings

Ant-lion ►
Name refers to larva which traps ants and other insects in a sandy hollow. Grabs them in its sickle-like jaws and sucks them dry. Not in Britain. Adult 35 mm long.

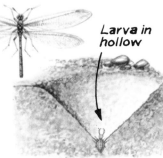

Larva in hollow

◄ Giant Lacewing
Mainly nocturnal. Larvae eat small midge larvae they find in wet moss at water's edge. Pupate in silken yellowish cocoons. 15 mm long.

Body length

Green Lacewing ►
Gardens and hedges and sometimes attracted to house lights. Weak fluttering flight. Larvae feed on aphids. 15 mm long.

Larva catching aphid

◄ Brown Lacewing
Smaller than Green Lacewing with dark brownish transparent wings. Near water in lush vegetation and on trees. Throughout Britain. 10 mm long.

Scorpion Fly, Alder Fly, Snake Fly

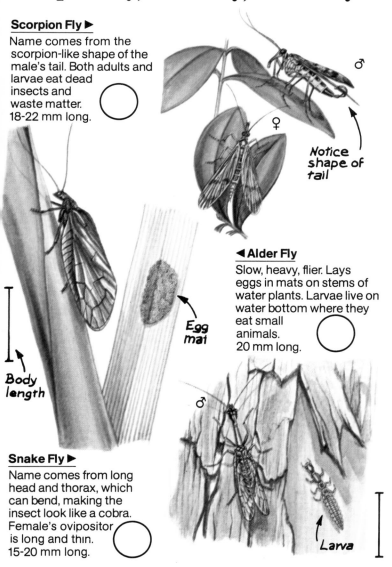

Scorpion Fly ▶
Name comes from the scorpion-like shape of the male's tail. Both adults and larvae eat dead insects and waste matter. 18-22 mm long.

♂

♀

Notice shape of tail

Body length

Egg mat

◀ Alder Fly
Slow, heavy, flier. Lays eggs in mats on stems of water plants. Larvae live on water bottom where they eat small animals. 20 mm long.

♂

Larva

Snake Fly ▶
Name comes from long head and thorax, which can bend, making the insect look like a cobra. Female's ovipositor is long and thin. 15-20 mm long.

Caddis Fly, Stonefly, Mayfly

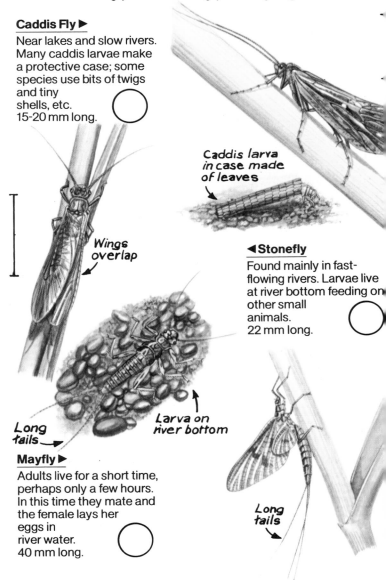

Caddis Fly ▶

Near lakes and slow rivers. Many caddis larvae make a protective case; some species use bits of twigs and tiny shells, etc.
15-20 mm long.

Caddis larva in case made of leaves

Wings overlap

◄ Stonefly

Found mainly in fast-flowing rivers. Larvae live at river bottom feeding on other small animals.
22 mm long.

Larva on river bottom

Long tails

Mayfly ▶

Adults live for a short time, perhaps only a few hours. In this time they mate and the female lays her eggs in river water.
40 mm long.

Long tails

Crickets

Crickets and bush crickets have very long antennae; grasshoppers' antennae are short. The third pair of legs on these insects is adapted for leaping. Males "sing" to attract females by rubbing their wing-cases together. The praying mantis, stick insect and cockroach belong to different orders.

Field Cricket ▶
Very rare. Grassy banks and meadows in sandy or chalky areas. Male sings from his burrow to attract a female.
Flightless.
20 mm long.

◀ House Cricket
In heated buildings and greenhouses. Also occurs in garden rubbish heaps and bigger tips.
Rarely flies.
Shrill song.
16 mm long.

Wood Cricket ▶
In leaf litter in woodland rides, ditches and banks in southern England. Male has quiet churring song. Flightless.
8-9 mm long.

◀ Mole Cricket
Burrows like a mole with its large spade-like fore-feet. Damp meadows. Male makes continuous whirring call.
Rare.
38-42 mm long.

Bush Crickets, Grasshopper

Great Green Bush Cricket ▶

Harsh, shrill, penetrating song. Moves slowly and never flies far. Eats small insects which it finds in dense vegetation. 45-47 mm long.

◀ Wart-biter

May bite when handled. Swedish people once used it to bite their warts. Coarse grassland on downs. Preys on small insects. 34-35 mm long.

Speckled Bush Cricket ▶

Flightless adults seen in late summer or early autumn. Found in old gardens where shrubs grow. Males' song is hard to hear. 11-13 mm long.

Long hind legs

Wings look silvery in flight

◀ Large Marsh Grasshopper

Local in bog and fenland in S. England, Norfolk Broads and Ireland. Flies a long way when disturbed. Male makes slow ticking song. 27-32 mm long.

Cockroaches, Mantis

Common Cockroach ▶

In houses and other warm buildings, where it eats waste. Female lays eggs in purse-like containers. Does not fly.
25 mm long.

Old bread

◀ German Cockroach

Not from Germany – it probably originated in N. Africa or the Middle East. In heated buildings.
13 mm long.

Dusky Cockroach ▶

Lives out-of-doors unlike its larger relatives. Found mainly in woodlands on leaves of trees.
7-10 mm long.

◀ Praying Mantis

Holds its forelegs together, as if praying, while waiting for its insect prey to come close. Scrub and tall grass in S. Europe.
Not in Britain.
60-80 mm long.

Stick Insect, Earwigs

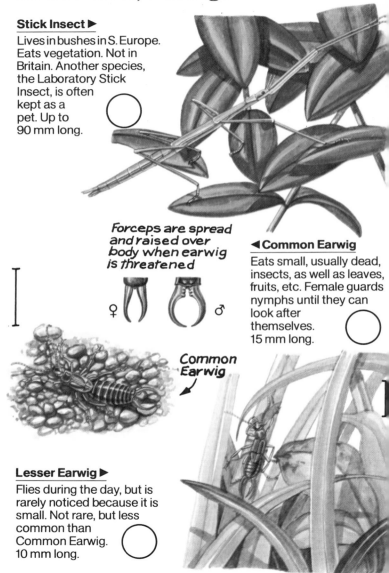

Stick Insect ▶

Lives in bushes in S. Europe. Eats vegetation. Not in Britain. Another species, the Laboratory Stick Insect, is often kept as a pet. Up to 90 mm long.

Forceps are spread and raised over body when earwig is threatened

♀ ♂

◀ Common Earwig

Eats small, usually dead, insects, as well as leaves, fruits, etc. Female guards nymphs until they can look after themselves. 15 mm long.

Common Earwig

Lesser Earwig ▶

Flies during the day, but is rarely noticed because it is small. Not rare, but less common than Common Earwig. 10 mm long.

Some other small insects

The insects on these pages are mostly very small and the pictures are greatly enlarged in some cases. The sizes given in the captions are very approximate. The insects shown here represent some of the other orders of insects not illustrated elsewhere in the book.

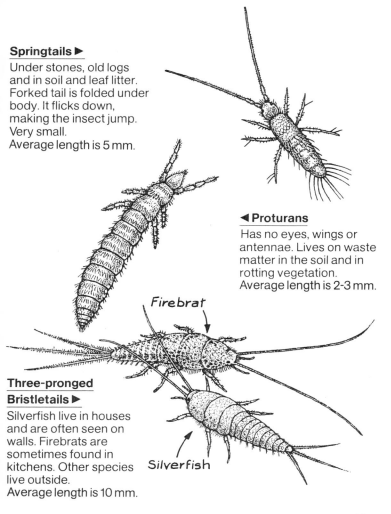

Springtails ▶
Under stones, old logs and in soil and leaf litter. Forked tail is folded under body. It flicks down, making the insect jump. Very small.
Average length is 5 mm.

◀ Proturans
Has no eyes, wings or antennae. Lives on waste matter in the soil and in rotting vegetation.
Average length is 2-3 mm.

Firebrat

Three-pronged Bristletails ▶
Silverfish live in houses and are often seen on walls. Firebrats are sometimes found in kitchens. Other species live outside.
Average length is 10 mm.

Silverfish

49

Two-pronged Bristletails ▶

Most live in soil. Some, like this one, are predators; others, like the white Campodea, are scavengers in the nests of ants, etc. Average length is 8 mm.

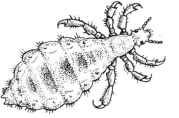

◀ Sucking Lice

These tiny insects live by sucking blood. Different species live on different animals, including people Average length is 2 mm.

Book and Bark Lice ▶

Some species in this group live outside on dead leaves, bark or in old birds' nests. Others live in old books and have no wings. Average length is 2 mm.

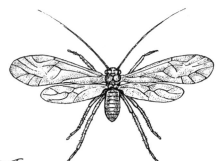

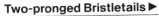

◀ Biting Lice

Live on birds and mammals, eating fragments of skin, hair, wool and feathers. No wings. Average length is 3 mm.

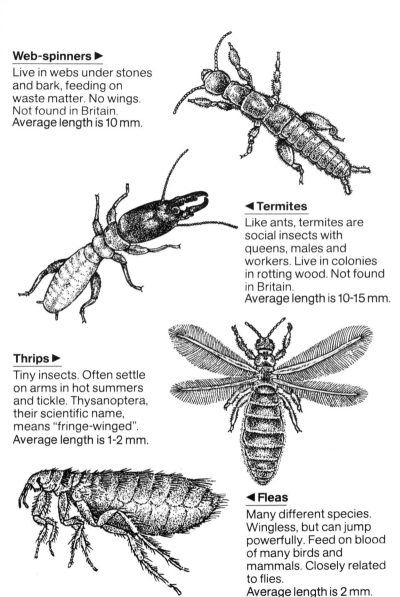

Web-spinners ▶

Live in webs under stones and bark, feeding on waste matter. No wings. Not found in Britain. **Average length is 10 mm.**

◀ Termites

Like ants, termites are social insects with queens, males and workers. Live in colonies in rotting wood. Not found in Britain. **Average length is 10-15 mm.**

Thrips ▶

Tiny insects. Often settle on arms in hot summers and tickle. Thysanoptera, their scientific name, means "fringe-winged". **Average length is 1-2 mm.**

◀ Fleas

Many different species. Wingless, but can jump powerfully. Feed on blood of many birds and mammals. Closely related to flies. **Average length is 2 mm.**

The insect life cycle

All insects lay eggs, but these do not usually hatch into adult insects. Some insects pass through two more stages before becoming adult. First the egg hatches into a larva which later becomes a pupa (or chrysalis). This process is called "complete metamorphosis." Bees, butterflies and beetles all change like this. The Seven-spot Ladybird shown here is an example.

The eggs of some insects, such as crickets, bugs and the dragonfly shown opposite, hatch into larvae called nymphs. Although they have no proper wings at first, nymphs grow into adult insects. They do not change into pupae. This is called "incomplete metamorphosis".

The adults of some insects only live for a very short time, but the metamorphosis may take years.

1

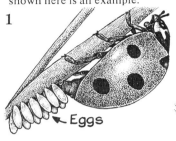

← Eggs

The female lays around 200 eggs in batches of two eggs up to about 50. She lays them under leaves and on plant stems where there are plenty of aphids for the larvae to feed on when they hatch. The eggs are yellow and shaped like skittles.

2

Larva   Aphids

In about a week the larva hatches, breaking the egg shell and pushing its way out. It is blue-grey with black and yellow markings. It eats hundreds of aphids, injecting them with digestive saliva and sucking up their insides as well as eating their solid parts.

3

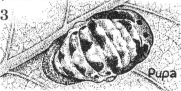

Pupa

The larva grows quickly. It grows a new skin and sheds its old one several times. When it reaches a certain size, it changes into a pupa. The pupa is encased in hard skin and attached to a leaf or stem by its tail. It does not move or eat. Inside its case, the pupa is becoming an adult ladybird.

4

Ladybirds mating

In about a week, the skin of the pupa splits and the fully-grown adult emerges. Adults continue to mate and lay eggs throughout the summer. In autumn, they hibernate often in large numbers, under bark in hedges or in houses or sheds

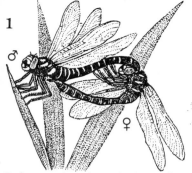

1

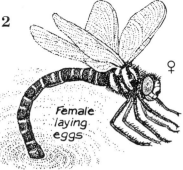

2

Female laying eggs

Before mating, the male dragonfly bends his tail up to transfer sperms to a special pairing organ on the second segment of his abdomen. He then straightens his body. During mating, he clasps the female by the back of the head with his tail claspers and the female brings up her body and places her abdomen in contact with the male's pairing organ.

Before and after mating, the pair often fly clasped together. This is called flying "in tandem".

The female then lays hundreds of eggs. Some dragonfly species drop the eggs into the water where they sink to the bottom. Others lay them in the stems of water plants or on floating weeds.

3

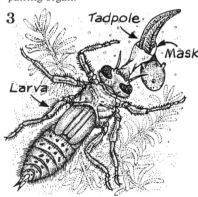

Tadpole

Mask

Larva

4 Adult emerging

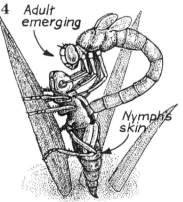

Nymph's skin

The eggs hatch out into nymphs which live either in mud on the water bed or among plants. They eat worms, small insects, such as mosquito larvae, and even small fishes and tadpoles. The nymph's large lower lip has two hooks on it. This "mask" can be shot out and the hooks used to catch prey.

The nymph lives for a year or more. As it grows it moults its skin several times. Before the final moult, the nymph crawls out of the water on to a plant stem. The skin splits along the back and the adult dragonfly emerges. Before flying away, it rests until its wings have expanded and its body has hardened. The adult lives for only about a month.

Food and feeding

Insects are carnivores (meat-eaters), herbivores (plant-eaters) or omnivores (animals that eat both meat and plants). Insects that live inside the bodies of other animals and feed on them are called parasites.

Insects' mouthparts are adapted in different ways to the food they eat. The strong jaws of certain beetles are used to catch and bite small animals; wasps gnaw soft-bodied insects and fruits with their cutting mouth parts, and can suck up liquids. Some insects, such as moths and butterflies, have a long tongue called a proboscis which they use for siphoning nectar from flowers. Bugs pierce plants and animals with a pointed rostrum. House-flies have a suction pad at the end of the proboscis. Saliva passes into the pad and partly digests food before it goes in the fly's mouth.

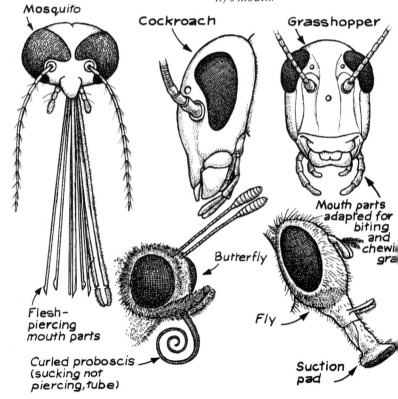

Mosquito

Cockroach

Grasshopper

Mouth parts adapted for biting and chewing grass

Flesh-piercing mouth parts

Butterfly

Curled proboscis (sucking not piercing, tube)

Fly

Suction pad

Defence

All insects are in constant danger of being eaten by birds, mammals, reptiles, amphibians, and other insects. These pictures show examples of their different methods of defending themselves.

Bee   Bombardier beetle   Ladybird   Cinnabar larva

Some insects, like ants and bees, sting or bite. Others produce nasty smells or poisons which shock the enemy and give the insect time to escape. The Bombardier Beetle "fires" a puff of toxic gas at its enemies.

Insects, like ladybirds, that taste unpleasant are often brightly coloured so that predators will avoid eating them. This is called "warning colouration". Birds learn not to eat these insects.

Wasp   Hover fly   Goat moth

Some harmless insects use warning colouration to copy the bright colours of bad tasting or poisonous insects. Wasp Beetles, for example, are the same colour as wasps. This is called "mimicry".

Camouflage is another method of defence. The colour of many insects makes them difficult for enemies to spot. Some moths have patterned wings that make them almost impossible to see on bark.

Stick Insect   Puss moth larva

Shape can also be a camouflage. Stick insects and some caterpillars, for example, resemble twigs so closely that they are safe from detection. Other insects look like leaves, grass or even seeds. Many play dead or freeze when threatened.

Some insects try to look as dangerous as possible when threatened. They may make sudden movements to frighten their enemies. The larva of the Puss Moth shows it its red face and waves its scarlet-tipped tails.

Keeping insects

If you want to study insects closely, you can keep them at home in a vivarium, although you should release the insects when you have made your study. Keep charts and records of their behaviour including feeding and breeding habits.

Collect insects in small tins, or test tubes which you can plug with cotton wool. Label the containers carefully and note when and where you find each species. Always take a sample of the plant you find each insect on – this is vital if you are collecting caterpillars, for example.

It is important to make the vivarium as like the insect's home as possible. A large sweet jar or an old fish tank covered in muslin or fine netting is suitable for most insects, and a converted shoebox will do for some species. Put soil or sand on the bottom as some insects like to bury themselves. Some also need drinking water, but make sure they cannot get drowned. Keep the vivarium away from direct sunlight, but not in a draught. Find out how your insects feed and feed them regularly with the right foods.

These are some of the insects you can keep. You can buy others, like stick insects, from pet shops.

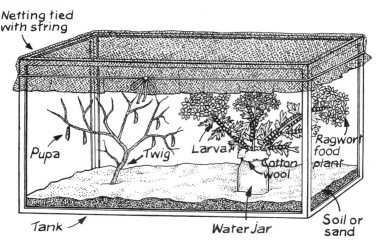

Netting tied with string

Pupa

Twig

Larva

Cotton wool

Ragwort food plant

Tank

Water Jar

Soil or sand

▲ Moths and butterflies

Moths and butterflies are easy to keep and their metamorphosis is fascinating to watch. You can find eggs, caterpillars or pupae in a wide variety of places such as on leaves, twigs or in the ground. If you collect caterpillars, you must take some of their food plant too and replace it with a fresh batch every day or two. Dig for moth pupae at the base of tree trunks that have grass growing in loose soil round them. You may not be able to identify the moth until it emerges.

Galls ▶

Collect galls from oak trees and rose bushes. Keep them in different jars and watch to see what comes out. Note down how many wasps or other insects come out of each gall and compare the time taken to emerge.

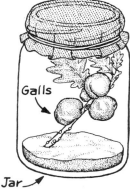

Galls

Jar

◀ Ladybirds and lacewings

Collect and keep some adult ladybirds and lacewings and you may be lucky enough to see their breeding process. Keep them in a box, a large jar or a tank. Make sure you have a plentiful supply of aphids to feed them on and put in fresh leaves regularly.

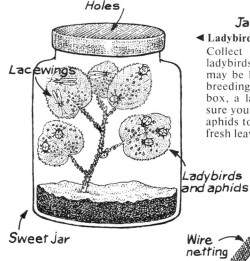

Holes

Lacewings

Ladybirds and aphids

Sweet Jar

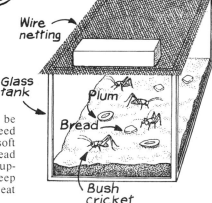

Wooden block

Wire netting

Glass tank

Plum

Bread

Bush cricket

Crickets and grasshoppers ▶

Crickets and grasshoppers can be kept in a fairly large glass tank. Feed crickets and bush crickets on soft bread, bits of fruit, lettuce and dead flies. Listen for the male's chirruping "song". You can also keep earwigs in this way as they will eat much the same food as crickets.

Glossary

Some of the definitions in this glossary refer specifically to insects, since they are the subject of this book. However, some of the words explained here could refer equally to other animals.

Abdomen – the hind section of an insect.
Algae – tiny water plants.
Antenna (plural: antennae) – most insects have a pair of antennae ("feelers") which they use for feeling and smelling.

Camouflage – when an insect's colour makes it difficult to see against its background.
Carnivorous – feeding on other animals.
Carrion – dead flesh. Some insects feed on the flesh of animals that have died or been left by carnivores.
Caste – social insects (eg. bees) consist of three castes (queens, drones and workers).
Chrysalis – see pupa.
Cocoon – a case which protects an insect pupa made by the larva before it pupates.
Colony – a group of insects which live together.
Compound eye – eye made up of many lenses.

Drone – male social insect.

Elytra (singular: elytron) – the wing covers of an insect (actually modified forewings).
Entomology – the study of insects.
Excrete – to get rid of waste from the body.

Food plant – a plant that an insect species feeds on.

Gall – a swelling on a plant caused by an insect larva.

Herbivorous – feeding only on plants.

Hibernation – when an insect spends the winter in a sleepy state.
Honeydew – a sweet liquid excreted by some insects and eaten by others.
Host – an insect that is attacked by a parasite.

Larva (plural: larvae) – a larva hatches from an insect's egg. This is also called the larval stage.
Local – insects that are found only in certain areas.

Mandibles – the biting, piercing and cutting mouthparts of an insect.
Metamorphosis – the process of changing from an egg to an adult, via a larva and (often) a pupa.
Mimicry – when an insect's shape or colour etc. copies that of another species, sometimes of a different order.
Moult – the shedding of an insect's skin during growth.

Nectar – a sweet-tasting liquid produced by flowers. Many insects feed on nectar.
Nocturnal – active at night.
Nymph – larva of an insect that does not pass through a pupal stage.
Omnivorous – feeding on both plants and animals.
Order – one of the scientific divisions of animals (eg. the order Diptera includes all true flies).
Ovipositor – a female insect's egg-laying organ.

Parasite – an insect that lives off another animal's body without giving anything in return.

Predator – an insect that kills and eats other animals.

Prey – an insect hunted by predators.

Proboscis – the long, tube-like "tongue" of some insects.

Pupa (plural: pupae) – the stage in an insect's life after the larval stage. The adult insect develops inside the pupa.

Queen – a female social insect which can lay eggs.

Reflex-bleeding – when an insect produces a liquid that looks like blood to frighten the enemy.

Rostrum – the long, tube-like stabbing mouthpart of bugs and weevils.

Scale-insect – a small, plant-sucking insect.

Scavenger – an insect that feeds on waste and dead matter.

Secrete – when an insect's body produces and gives off a chemical from a gland.

Social insects – insects that live in colonies and are organized so that each of the three castes have different duties.

Species – a group of insects that can breed together.

Stridulation – method of making sound used by insects like crickets and grasshoppers where one part of the body is rubbed against another.

Thorax – the middle section of an insect to which the legs and wings are attached.

Worker – female social insect that cannot breed. These insects work for the colony.

Clubs to join

British Entomological & Natural History Society
Studies particularly entomology and insect conservation. Holds weekly meetings, summer field meetings and an annual exhibition. Owns collections and a library. Address: C/o Alpine Club, 74, South Audley Street, London W1.

Amateur Entomologists' Society
Holds meetings and exhibitions and publishes a quarterly bulletin as well as useful pamphlets and leaflets. Address: 355, Hounslow Road, Hansworth, Feltham, Middx.

British Naturalists' Association
Holds regular field and indoor meetings for studying natural history, including insects. Their magazine has regular articles about insects and a special junior section. Address: Thorneyholme Hall, Roughlee, near Burnley, Lancs. BB12 9LH.

Books to read

The NatureTrail Book of Insect Watching. Thomson (Usborne).
A Field Guide to the Insects of Britain and Northern Europe. Chinery (Collins)
Insects in Colour. Sandhall (Lutterworth Press)
Insects and their world, Oldroyd (British Museum (Natural History))
Insects are animals, too. Wootton (David & Charles)
Discovering Garden Insects. Wootton (Shire)
The Insects in Your Garden. Oldroyd (Puffin)
Insect Natural History. Imms (Collins New Naturalist series)
Studying Insects. Ford (Warne)
The Oxford Book of Insects. Burton (Oxford)
Spotter's Guide to Butterflies. Hyde (Usborne)
Spotter's Guide to Wild Flowers. Humphries (Usborne) will help you identify insects' food plants.

Scorecard

The insects in this scorecard are arranged in alphabetical order. When you spot an insect, fill in the date next to its name. You can add up your score after a day out spotting.

	Score	Date seen		Score	Date seen
Agrion, Banded	15		Beetle, Devil's Coach Horse	5	
Agrion, Demoiselle	15		Beetle, Dor	10	
Alder Fly	5		Beetle, Great Diving	10	
Ant, Black	5		Beetle, Great Silver Water	15	
Ant, Carpenter	25		Beetle, Green Tiger	10	
Ant, Red	5		Beetle, Green Tortoise	10	
Ant, Wood	10		Beetle, Horned Dung	15	
Ant, Yellow Meadow	5		Beetle, Large Green Ground	20	
Ant-lion	25		Beetle, Musk	15	
Aphid, Bean	5		Beetle, Oil	15	
Aphid, Rose	5		Beetle, Red and Black Burying	10	
Bee, Leaf-cutter	15		Beetle, Rove	15	
Beetle, Ant	15		Beetle, Scarlet-tipped Flower	10	
Beetle, Bee	20		Beetle Stag	15	
Beetle, Blister	25		Beetle, Violet Ground	5	
Beetle, Bloody-nosed	15		Beetle, Wasp	10	
Beetle, Bombardier	15		Beetle, Water	10	
Beetle, Cardinal	10		Beetle, Whirligig	5	
Beetle, Click	15		Blue, Holly	10	
Beetle, Colorado	25		Brimstone	10	
Beetle, Death Watch	15		Brown, Wall	10	

	Score	Date seen		Score	Date seen
Bug, Forest	10		Fly, Bee	10	
Bug, Heath Assassin	10		Fly, Drone	10	
Bug, Saucer	10		Fly, Dung	5	
Bumblebee, Red-tailed	5		Fly, Fever	5	
Bush Cricket, Great Green	15		Fly, Greenbottle	5	
Bush Cricket, Speckled	10		Fly, Grey Flesh	5	
Caddis Fly	10		Fly, Horse	15	
Chafer, Rose	15		Fly, Hover	10	
Cicada, New Forest	25		Fly, Robber	15	
Cicada, Southern	25		Fritillary, Pearl-bordered	15	
Cockchafer	5		Froghopper, Black and Red	10	
Cockroach, Common	5		Gall-wasp, Oak Apple (or gall)	5	
Cockroach, Dusky	15		Gall-wasp, Oak Marble (or gall)	5	
Cockroach, German	10		Glow-worm	15	
Cranefly, Black and Yellow	10		Glow-worm, Lesser	25	
Cranefly, Giant	10		Gnat, Common	5	
Cricket, Field	25		Grasshopper, Large Marsh	20	
Cricket, House	15		Hairstreak, Purple	15	
Cricket, Mole	25		Hawk Moth, Death's Head	25	
Cricket, Wood	15		Hawk Moth, Elephant	15	
Downy Emerald	15		Hawk Moth, Eyed	10	
Dragonfly, Emperor	15		Hawk Moth, Hummingbird	15	
Dragonfly, Golden-ringed	10		Hawk Moth, Lime	10	
Earwig, Common	5		Hawk Moth, Poplar	10	
Earwig, Lesser	15		Hawk Moth, Privet	15	

	Score	Date seen		Score	Date seen
Hornet	20		Moth, Herald	10	
Horntail, Blue	15		Moth, Lappet	15	
Ichneumon Fly	15		Moth, Lobster	15	
Ischnura, Common	5		Moth, Merveille-du-Jour	15	
Lacewing, Brown	10		Moth, Mother Shipton	10	
Lacewing, Giant	15		Moth, Oak Eggar	15	
Lacewing, Green	5		Moth, Peach Blossom	10	
Ladybird, Eyed	15		Moth, Puss	10	
Ladybird, 14-spot	10		Moth, Red Underwing	15	
Ladybird, Seven-spot	5		Moth, Silver Y	10	
Ladybird, 22-spot	10		Moth, Six-spot Burnet	5	
Ladybird, Two-spot	5		Moth, Swallow-tailed	10	
Leafhopper, Eared	20		Moth, Vapourer	5	
Leafhopper, Green	10		Moth, Wood Tiger	15	
Libellula, Broad-bodied	10		Moth, Yellow-tail	5	
Mantis, Praying	25		Peacock	5	
Mayfly	10		Pond Skater	5	
Moth, Alder	20		Sawfly, Birch	10	
Moth, Cinnabar	10		Scorpion Fly	5	
Moth, Clifden Nonpareil	25		Shieldbug, Green	10	
Moth, Emperor	15		Shieldbug, Pied	10	
Moth, Forester	15		Snake Fly	15	
Moth, Garden Tiger	5		Stick Insect	25	
Moth, Ghost	5		Stonefly	10	
Moth, Goat	15		Sympetrum, Ruddy	15	

	Score	Date seen		Score	Date seen
Treehopper, Horned	15		Water Boatman	10	
Velvet Ant	15		Water Boatman, Lesser	10	
Wart-biter	25		Water Cricket	10	
Wasp, German	5		Water Measurer	10	
Wasp, Giant Wood	15		Water Scorpion	15	
Wasp, Potter	15		Water Stick Insect	15	
Wasp, Ruby-tailed	10		Weevil, Nut	5	
Wasp, Sand	10		White, Marbled	15	
Wasp, Tree	10		Yellow, Clouded	15	

Index